Victoria M. Howard

Junior

THE RACEHORSE THAT WON THE KENTUCKY DERBY

AuthorHouse™
1663 Liberty Drive
Bloomington, IN 47403
www.authorhouse.com
Phone: 1 (800) 839-8640

Published by AuthorHouse 02/07/2018

ISBN: 978-1-5462-2848-6 (sc)
978-1-5462-2849-3 (e)

Library of Congress Control Number: 2018901796

Print information available on the last page.

authorHOUSE®

(For children of all ages)

To California Chrome—the richest racehorse in history

Contents

A Colt Is Born

It was February 18, 2011. It was a rainy day at Harris
Farms in California.

A mare named Love the Chase was lying in her
thick bed of straw. She was about to give birth to her
first baby.

It takes a horse almost one year to have a foal. A foal
is what a baby horse is called.

Love the Chase was a thoroughbred racehorse that
was owned by Steve and Carolyn Coburn and Perry and
Denise Martin.

They loved their horse very much. When Love the Chase couldn't race anymore they decided to breed her. The reason she couldn't race was because she had a breathing problem.

Her owners chose a stallion named Lucky Pulpit to be the sire of the foal.

A sire is what the father of a baby horse is called.

A dam is what the mother of a baby horse is called.

The Martins and Coburns hoped that with a name like Lucky Pulpit they would get lucky and have a beautiful, healthy baby horse.

Soon her water broke, and Love the Chase had

her baby.

It was a boy—a BIG BOY!

A normal baby horse weighs around one hundred

pounds when it is born.

But Love the Chase's baby weighed 135 pounds.

"You better call the Coburns and Martins and tell

them they are proud parents of a beautiful chestnut

colt," the veterinarian said.

A Difficult Labor

Because the foal was so big as he came through the
birth canal, he tore the inside of his mother. The
veterinarian had to give Love the Chase stitches and
medicine.

Love the Chase was in a lot of pain and didn't want
to be bothered with her baby.

The newborn colt tried to stand up. It usually takes
foals several times before they can stand, for their legs
are wobbly.

After the colt was up on all four legs, it wasn't long
before he started running circles around his momma.
"Boy, this is one feisty horse. And he is fast!" the
veterinarian said.
The girls who worked in the barn immediately fell in
love with the sweet colt. They smothered the colt with
kisses and took turns scratching his neck.
The colt loved all the attention and loved having his
neck scratched.

When Steve Coburn and his wife arrived at the barn

and saw what a gorgeous colt Love the Chase had, they

were thrilled.

"You know, I think we just might have our first

Kentucky Derby winner," Steve told Carolyn.

"That would be great. But you know how hard it is

to own a horse that wins the Kentucky Derby?" asked

Carolyn.

"I know, but I feel lucky. This colt is special. I can feel

it!" Steve said.

We Will Call You Junior

"What are we going to call you, little one?" asked Steve.

After he thought about it for a minute, he said, "I think we will call you Junior for now. That's because you look so much like your daddy, Lucky Pulpit. Of course, we will need to give you a real racehorse name later on. One that you will be proud of."

The colt had many admirers for he was strikingly handsome. He was chestnut in color and had four white stockings and a long white blaze on his face.

He was very sweet and loved people. Because there were always people around him, he became a "people" horse.

After about a month, Love the Chase was better and now ready to go outside in the field and play with her son. The mother and son loved being outside in the large pasture. They would run and play, kicking their heels up. Being outside and running makes a young horse strong. For the next six months, the mare and colt enjoyed their life together under the California sun.

Playing in the Pasture
with New Friends

When baby horses are small, they play in the

pasture together.

The girl horses are called fillies, and the boy horses

are called colts. The fillies and colts are usually separated

and put into different paddocks.

Their mothers stay close by to watch them and

make sure they don't get into trouble, like most young

baby animals do.

They can get very frisky, chasing one another and

jumping on each other's back.

They eat grass, lie down in the sun, and chase one another all day.

At night, they are usually brought inside the barn where they each have their own special stall, which is their home.

They nurse their mothers to get the milk they need, which is so important to make their bones strong.

Baby horses get their first set of teeth before they are even born.

This is so they can start eating grain, hay, and grass by the time they are several weeks old.

Baby horses usually nurse until they are six months

of age.

About this time they are taken away, which is

called weaning.

This is a sad time for the babies as they are taken

away and put someplace where they cannot see or hear

their mothers.

They will cry for a few days, but then they will stop.

Usually they will buddy up with another colt or filly

that will become their special friend.

Getting a New Name

Picking a name for their four-legged child was not easy

for the Coburns and Martins.

They all had a different name that they liked.

Carolyn Coburn wanted the name Lucky at Love.

Her husband Steve liked the name California

Chrome. (The white markings on a horse is known as

chrome, and the horse and owners came from the state

of California.)

Denise Martin liked the name Big Chapter, and her

husband Perry chose the name Seabisquik.

Because they all liked different names, they wrote

down their choices on a piece of paper and threw them

into Steve's cowboy hat.

They were at a restaurant and asked a waitress to

pull a name out of Steve's hat.

The waitress pulled out the paper that said

California Chrome.

When they went to the barn later that day, they

told Junior, "Your new race name is going to be

CALIFORNIA CHROME."

As if he understood what they said, he lifted his head

up and nickered as he smiled.

"I think Junior likes his new name." Carolyn laughed.

Training to Race

California Chrome grew to be a beautiful horse. He was

now one year old (called a yearling).

It was now time to start training him to race. That is

what racehorses are born to do.

His owners sent California Chrome to a

trainer named Alan Sherman, who was a very

good horse trainer.

Every day Alan would put a saddle on California

Chrome's back and a bridle in his mouth so he could get

used to it.

Next, the exercise rider got on California Chrome's

back and would lead him around the barn and then the

racetrack.

The trainer was very pleased with his new student.

California Chrome did everything just the way Alan

wanted him to.

After several weeks of exercising the horse,

California Chrome and his rider went behind the

starting gate.

After several months of training, Alan thought

California Chrome was ready to race.

California Chrome's First Baby Race

It was April 26, 2013.

It was the day when California Chrome would run

his very first race.

His owners, the Martins and the Coburns, were at

the racetrack to watch their baby.

They looked like proud parents but were very nervous.

When the race was over, California Chrome

finished second.

Everyone was happy. When they got back to the

barn, they gave the horse lots of hugs and kisses.

Carolyn brought her horse his very favorite treat—a

bag of Mrs. Pastures Cookies for Horses.

When California Chrome heard the bag open, he ran

to the front of the stall.

"I am so proud of you. I brought you a bag of your favorite cookies. You did so good today you can eat the whole bag," said Carolyn.

Everyone laughed as the horse put his mouth into the bag and chomped away.

Winning the Kentucky Derby

The big day had arrived. It was May 3, 2014.

It was the day that millions of people around the

world had been waiting for.

There were thousands of racing fans at Churchill

Downs in Kentucky. It was the 140th year that a

Kentucky Derby was run.

The Kentucky Derby is like the Super Bowl of

horse racing.

A horse that wins the Derby will be written in the history books as one of the best racehorses ever. The television cameras were rolling as nineteen three-year-old thoroughbreds took their position behind the starting gate.

California Chrome moved into his assigned position—number 5.

When the bell rang, the horses took off. California Chrome got away third, then fell back to fourth.

At the top of the stretch, California Chrome soared ahead of the other horses, winning the race by one and three-fourths lengths.

As he passed the fans, Jockey Victor Espinoza held

his whip in the air as he smiled at the people.

In the winner's circle, the garland of 554 roses was

carefully placed over California Chrome's back.

Everyone was hugging the winning horse—even

Victor Espinoza.

When California Chrome got back to the barn, his

owners were waiting for him.

As the proud champion walked into his stall, they

cheered and opened bags of his favorite snack—Mrs.

Pastures Cookies.

As he was devouring his treats, Steve Coburn said, "I

always knew you were a champion."

Other Books by Victoria M. Howard

Children's Books:

The Adventures of Max

Book 1: The Adventures of Max and Molly

Book 2: Max Goes to School

Book 3: Max and His Friends Save the World

Book 4: The Birth of a Racehorse

Book 5: The Stairway to Heaven

Junior: The Racehorse That Won the Kentucky Derby

Adult Books:

Why Women Love Bad Boys

Dating Over 50

This One's for the Boys

I Am Woman

The Butterfly Effect

The Evolution of Angie

Horse Books:

Roosevelt Raceway: Where It All Began

(with Haughton and Hudson)

Meadow Skipper: The Untold Story

(with Bob Marks)

Murray Brown: Book Full and Closed

www.ingramcontent.com/pod-product-compliance
Lightning Source LLC
Chambersburg PA
CBHW041132280526
45792CB00013B/2389